# THE JAMES BACKHOUSE LECTURES

T0363949

This is one of a series of annual lectures which began in 1964 when Australia Yearly Meeting of the Religious Society of Friends was first established.

The lecture is named after James Backhouse, who travelled with his companion George Washington Walker throughout the Australian colonies from 1832 to 1838.

Backhouse and Walker were English Quakers who came to Australia with a particular concern for social justice. Having connections to social reform movements in the early colonies as well as in Britain, Backhouse and Walker planned to record their observations and make recommendations for positive change where needed.

Detailed observations were made of all the prisons and institutions visited by Backhouse and Walker. Their reports, submitted to local as well as British authorities, made recommendations for legislative reform. Many of the changes they initiated resulted in improvements to the health and wellbeing of convicts, Aboriginal people and the general population.

A naturalist and a botanist, James Backhouse is remembered also for his detailed accounts of native vegetation which were later published.

James Backhouse was welcomed by isolated communities and Friends throughout the colonies. He shared with all his concern for social justice and encouraged others in their faith. A number of Quaker meetings began as a result of his visit.

Australian Friends hope that these lectures, which reflect the experiences and ongoing concerns of Friends, may offer fresh insight and be a source of inspiration.

The 2023 Backhouse Lecture *Quakers, the Internet, and What's Next* was delivered by Jon Watts, song writer and multimedia artist, via Zoom on Tuesday 4th July, 2023. Jon is from Central Philadelphia Monthly Meeting.

The lecture recounts his interesting spiritual journey from a Quaker family in Virginia and discovering inspirational stories of early Friends at Guildford College to a vocation in media.

An early You Tube music video of his, *Dance Party Erupts in Quaker Meeting for Worship*, went viral and led to a "light-bulb moment" and the idea to create weekly Quaker Speak videos. As many of us know the videos have great potential for o reach and "inreach".

Jon Watts challenges us in these troubled times to find our Qu er voice and to let the Spirit be heard via the internet, as well as in person. We all ha different skills and aptitudes but we can share from that place of deep listening and s tual inspiration and help to create the beloved community here on earth.

Bruce Henry,
Presiding Clerk,
Australia Yearly Meeting
July 2023

# THE JAMES BACKHOUSE LECTURES

2002 *To Do Justly, and to Love Mercy: Learning from Quaker Service*, Mark Deasey

2003 *Respecting the Rights of Children and Young People: A New Perspective on Quaker Faith and Practice*, Helen Bayes

2004 *Growing Fruitful Friendship: A Garden Walk*, Ute Caspers

2005 *Peace is a Struggle*, David Johnson

2006 *One Heart and a Wrong Spirit: The Religious Society of Friends and Colonial Racism*, Polly O Walker

2007 *Support for Our True Selves: Nurturing the Space Where Leadings Flow*, Jenny Spinks

2008 *Faith, Hope and Doubt in Times of Uncertainty: Combining the Realms of Scientific and Spiritual Inquiry*, George Ellis

2009 *The Quaking Meeting: Transforming Our Selves, Our Meetings and the More than-human World*, Helen Gould

2010 *Finding our voice: Our truth, community and journey as Australian Young Friends*, Australian Young Friends

2011 *A demanding and uncertain adventure: Exploration of a concern for Earth restoration and how we must live to pass on to our children*, Rosemary Morrow

2012 *From the inside out: Observations on Quaker work at the United Nations*, David Atwood

2013 *A Quaker astronomer reflects: Can a scientist also be religious?* Jocelyn Bell Burnell

2014 *'Our life is love, and peace, and tenderness': Bringing children into the centre of Quaker life and worship*, Tracy Bourne

2015 *'This we can do': Quaker faith in action through the Alternatives to Violence Project*, Sally Herzfeld

2016 *Everyday prophets*, Margery Post Abbott

2017 *Reflections on the 50th anniversary of the 1967 Referendum in the context of two Aboriginal life stories*, David Carline and Cheryl Buchanan

2018 *An Encounter between Quaker Mysticism and Taoism in Everyday Life*, Cho-Nyon Kim

2019 *Animating freedom: Accompanying Indigenous struggles for self-determination*, Jason MacLeod

2020 *Seeking union with spirit: Experiences of spiritual journeys*, Fiona Gardner

2022 *Creating hope: Working for justice in catastrophic times*, Yarrow Goodley

# 2023

THE **JAMES BACKHOUSE** LECTURE

How My 2009 Viral Video

Transformed My Perspective on

# Quakers,
# the Internet,
# and
# What's Next

## JON WATTS

Quakers
AUSTRALIA

ISBN 978-1922830-09-8 (PB); ISBN 978-1922830-10-4 (eBk)

The moral rights of the author have been asserted.

**Design & layout by:**
Interactive Publications, Carindale, Queensland, Australia

**Cover image:** supplied by the author.

A catalogue record for this book is available from the National Library of Australia

# Contents

# About the author

Jon Watts is a Quaker songwriter and multimedia artist. As a songwriter, Jon has toured the world sharing stories of the Early Friends and his own spiritual journey growing up Quaker in Virginia and attending the Quaker Leadership Scholars Program at Guilford College.

Jon's unique success promoting his music in the early days of YouTube led him to found the QuakerSpeak project, for which he spent six years travelling, interviewing Friends, and publishing a video every week. In 2021, Jon embarked on a new journey: envisioning a future for Friends and online media.

Jon Watts is a member of Central Philadelphia Monthly Meeting, which holds his ministry under its care. He lives in Germantown, where he enjoys hiking in the Wissahickon with his wife and recording music in his home studio.

# Introduction

So all you Friends in the Meeting house
put your hands up
and then twist them at the wrist
like you just got out of handcuffs
that's how you clap for me
you've got to clap silently
– "Friend Speaks My Mind", 2007

In 2007, I wrote an autobiographical song about growing up as a Quaker. Called "Friend Speaks My Mind", the song, an upbeat exploration of an adolescence spent at youth groups and summer camps, was an earnest attempt at theological reckoning intermingled with some friendly inside jokes.

A few years later I filmed a short music video at Pendle Hill, a Quaker retreat center near Philadelphia, to promote the song. The concept was a Quaker Meeting for Worship that transforms into a dance party after I stand and deliver the song as vocal ministry. When it was finished, I uploaded the video to a brand-new online video platform called YouTube.

For those of us who remember that era, the idea of online video streaming was very new. We were still receiving DVDs in the mail! So, the concept of online video streaming was novel, even more so a platform where anyone with a camera and an internet connection could post a video for the world to see. Looking back, it seems trite (we were so innocent!), but at the time it was mind-boggling.

My own YouTube channel, which I had just launched the year before, had three videos and a couple hundred views. I was feeling good. So I uploaded this new music video, named it *Dance party erupts in Quaker Meeting for Worship*, sent it out to the handful of people on my newsletter list, and left for a camping trip.

When I returned a few days later, I checked the video. It had 30,000 views. My inbox was full of messages from Quakers all over the world, including places where I hadn't realized Quakers existed. I was stunned. At the time, the term "viral video" had not yet been coined. There was no road map for how to navigate this amount of sudden attention, and it wasn't all

*1*

glowing. The comments section was full of Quakers from around the globe passionately—and often rudely—disagreeing with one another about the theology in the lyrics.

Some commenters said they loved the video, while others hated it. Some were saying, 'I've never even heard of this kind of Quaker', while others said, 'I've only ever heard of this kind of Quaker.' They seemed deeply frustrated with each other, as if to ask, 'What kind of bubble are you in?'

To make matters more interesting, there was a third category of people, who left comments like, 'I've never heard of Quakerism *at all* but it looks pretty fun. I'd like to try it out.' Of course, that was not my reason for making the video, but processing the whirlwind of attention, positivity, negativity, and sincere curiosity, a light bulb turned on for me.

Here's the light bulb: we have crossed into a new era where we are encountering each other across theological lines and geographic lines in ways that our spiritual ancestors never did. Our carefully built Quaker silos have fallen, for better or for worse.

At the same time, seekers and newcomers have unprecedented access, not only to information about the Quaker spiritual path but also to the dialogues happening inside our communities—our dramas and our disagreements. This is new territory. There is no precedent.[1]

My epiphany in 2009 has guided my work up to this day, and I'm honored to have this opportunity through the Backhouse Lecture to explore that light-bulb moment: What are the pitfalls and challenges of this new era of connectedness? What are the opportunities newly available with these 21st-century platforms? How is the Spirit calling us forth? What's next?

---

[1] Or is there?

# Part 1: Growing up Quaker

Please bear with me as I rewind the clock for a moment in order to establish some context. Join me for a (brief) visit to the 1990s.

## Growing up in an intentional Quaker community

My parents joined the Quaker Meeting in Richmond, Virginia, a few years before I was born. They had both grown up Catholic. They knew they were done with it, but didn't know what was next. When they attended a Quaker wedding, they fell in love with Quakerism. When someone in the Richmond Friends Meeting bought a piece of property outside the city and invited members of the Meeting to join them in an intentional community, my parents signed up.

When I was four years old, we built our house in Ashland Vineyard, along with five other families from Richmond Meeting. I grew up attending community dinners, playing with the other kids in the community and Richmond Meeting, and exploring the expansive property upon which Ashland Vineyard was located. Every household had an open-door policy, and I felt nurtured, mentored and cared for by all six sets of parents.

If I were required to name the core theological tenets of the community, I would find it difficult. It was not something we often discussed, if at all. Maybe most felt it was a private matter, or perhaps there was no cohesive shared understanding. Our meetings began and ended in silence. We had a practice of silence before meals, and we shared a core value of 'do no harm' when it came to the social fabric of the community. Compared with the home life of many of my school peers, these were radical practices; I cannot count all the ways I benefited from this unique upbringing.

## Summers at camp

By the time I was 11, I was spending my summers at Camp Shiloh in the Appalachian Mountains, where I learned to hike and canoe and rock climb. Between Shiloh and another camp called Catoctin, I had the most magical summertime community one could dream of. We slept outside, told each other everything, and we kept in touch throughout the year. I had my first kiss, learned to play guitar, and experienced the most meaningful worship I have ever had in my life—while around a campfire with the open night sky above us.

It was at camp that I learned how to quiet my mind and how to wait on the Spirit to move me to speak in a worship sharing, and, perhaps most importantly, I learned that the Spirit could choose anyone. Whether you were the director of the camp or an eight-year-old visiting your older sibling for the day, it didn't matter—your voice was welcome (and could be powerful) in that space.

# Young Friends

A few camp friends invited me to the Baltimore Yearly Meeting Young Friends conferences, where up to 100 high school age Quakers would descend on a Meeting house, cover the floor with sleeping bags and spend the weekend laughing, playing music, cooking, and conducting our community business in the way that only Young Friends can: in a giant cuddle puddle on the ground.

Unlike my public high school experience, when I was at a Young Friends conference, I had agency. I was responsible for my own community. Along with my peers, I wrote epistles that were read at the Yearly Meeting. We set the guidelines for conferences and confronted our Friends when they didn't honor those guidelines.

My sense of possibility for Quakers in the world felt expansive—almost overwhelming. Every conference seemed to attract more and more people. Everyone was telling their friends about this magical space where young people had agency and power. And yet this was just one small corner of the world. Imagine if groups of young people everywhere were gathering this way, finding solidarity with their peers and calling out their elders when the world they inherited fails to align with what feels so clearly possible. We might just start pulling down the pillars of this world, so fundamentally infused with empire, and transforming it into a more connected, loving and just place.

Again, the theology of the group was not explicit. We worshiped in silence, conducted business in the manner of Friends and upheld the wellness of the community as a whole. If theology did come up in these conferences, it was usually as a joke or as a response to the mainstream evangelical Christian movement, whose politics we opposed. Either way, it didn't matter to me. I felt more connected to those Friends and to the Spirit than I have at many other periods in my life, and I was deeply content.

When my high school days ended and it came time to choose a college, I had just one criterion: how can I continue this thread of spiritual intimacy and Quaker community? I didn't have to look far.

# Part 2: Guilford College

The Quaker Leadership Scholars Program at Guilford College in North Carolina promised a continuation of the close Quaker community experience of my youth, and I was all in. What I didn't know was that the founder of the program, Max Carter, had crafted the program to expose those Quakers who had grown up in a theological bubble to branches and beliefs they did not yet know existed.

Max Carter was hard to miss at Guilford. Sporting a straw hat, collarless shirt and long gray beard, Max would ride his bicycle around campus and invite students into his spiritual oasis—"the hut!"—in the middle of campus. There was always a fire roaring in the hut, and fresh tea or coffee available. Despite having never met a Quaker like Max—that is, a plain-dressed, holiness-influenced Indiana Friend—I was put at ease by his friendly, welcoming demeanor and gentle, playful humor.

On my first day at Guilford College, however, Max took us on a field trip to an evangelical Friends church. It had a pulpit and a pastor and a Christian flag and no cuddle puddles. I began talking with my fellow students in the program and realized their beliefs and backgrounds were really different from mine. My head was spinning. How could we all call ourselves Quakers when we were so different from each other? More to the point: how could these Jesus-loving, loud, southern, conservative Christians belong to the same progressive, silence-loving faith in which I had grown up? I came to the conclusion that someone was a fraud; either they were fakers, or I was. How could we all be Friends?

This was a dangerous conclusion for me to draw. Doubt began to creep in. Was it possible that I was the one in the wrong? My peers were equally aghast at some of the aspects of my Quaker upbringing and identity. I didn't use Christian language. I had no working definition of the word God and no clear relationship with the concept of Christ. I had never read the Bible. My primary spiritual concern, it seemed, was with building a healthy community. I began to feel that they might be right about something.

One of the tremendous gifts of the Quaker Leadership Scholars Program was the abundance of seasoned, patient mentors and elders. I approached one of my mentors, the director at the time of the Quaker Leadership Scholars Program, Scott Pierce Coleman, with my concerns. He listened to my challenges and asked me a few questions. He asked me about my personal spiritual practice as a Quaker, about my relationship with God. Hearing that I had no meaningful answers for either of these two questions, my trusted mentor offered that perhaps it was true: there was no place for me in the Religious Society of Friends. I was crushed. I experienced a serious crisis of faith. For a time, I left Quakerism. I dropped out of Guilford to take a day job and work on songwriting. Although it was a relief to take a break from those existential questions about my faith and upbringing, I felt something was missing. I experienced an inward pull to return to the conversation, to go deeper.

When I returned to Guilford, I felt "brought low", as we say among Friends. I knew that I didn't know. I also knew that despite my commitment to the Quaker community, something was missing from my own personal practice of this religious tradition. I set out on a mission to figure out what it was. The year was 2006.

Humbly, on my knees, I returned to my mentor, Max Carter, and I said, 'Max, please tell me the stories of the early Quakers.' If you have ever had the privilege of meeting Max, you know that that is the question he has been waiting for his whole life. His stories spilled forth, one after the other. Through Max's telling, I was surprised to discover some of my favorite stories in the whole world.

Max told me the story of George Fox and Margaret Fell. He told me stories of Mary Fisher and Mary Dyer, Levi Coffin and Lucretia Mott, stories of John Woolman and Benjamin Lay. He told me some lesser-known stories, such as that of Solomon Eccles and of James Nayler, the Quaker who rode into the city of Bristol in a re-enactment of Jesus's triumphal entry into Jerusalem and was whipped through the streets of London and back, and branded on his forehead with a "B" for blasphemer.

As I took in these amazing, moving, confounding stories of the early Quakers, I needed to find a way to process them. I did what I had always done to process powerfully emotional experiences: I began to write songs.

> James Nayler hadn't slept for days. He had a letter in his pocket from George and Margaret Fell they prayed that he would read in time to stop it. They eldered him. He would respect them. And not Martha Simmons.
> – "Another Naylor Sonnet", 2006

Why were these stories so captivating to me? One word: shenanigans. Stick with me …

From running naked through the streets of 17th-century England, to interrupting Sunday church services by marching down the aisles with shoe-cobbling materials, to gathering up violins and musical manuscripts and setting them on fire in a public square in London, the early Friends were anything but subtle.[2]

If you are a collector of interesting, weird, dramatic stories (as I am), upon hearing of the early Friends, you may feel (as I do) that you have struck gold. These 17th-century religious radicals were creative, bold, confrontational and more than a little risky. The stories of their public shenanigans are weird, baffling and often ridiculous. But even better: these stories can be inspiring.

In this current era as we watch political leaders and other elites abuse their power and hurt those around them, the rest of the species, and the natural world, what are we to do? We don't have a seat at the table. Often, we feel powerless.

The early Quakers turned this question on its head: What is power? What is stopping us from walking around the world challenging worldly authority and claiming our own spiritual power as equally valid? They confronted the society around them and those in positions of political authority in bombastic, eye-catching and ultimately effective ways. But their shenanigans were not without incredible risk.

For my part, I came into the process of writing these songs about the early Friends feeling so broken open, so open-hearted and so ready to learn that they didn't feel like ancient strangers from long ago. These are my spiritual ancestors. As their hopes and dreams are my hopes and dreams, so is their suffering my suffering. When I came to the part in the story where James Nayler was whipped through the streets of London, I wept. I wept in solidarity with this man, whom I thought of as courageous and perhaps a bit foolish but a genuinely earnest seeker of truth, peace and justice. I wept at the unfairness of how his people—my people—were treated in their society. And I wept at their willingness to put everything on the line, to risk life and limb to remake society into the beloved community according to the blueprints laid out in the Sermon on the Mount.

And something clicked. This faith tradition is about more than community. It's about more than silence. It's about more than peace, even. The Quaker faith is about deep trust. It's about deep listening. It is about doing the hard and courageous thing and opening our hearts to the spotlight of transformation. And it's about doing that together. But there is another step.

---

[2] All three of these stories were sourced from just one early Friend.

Quaker practice is about being stripped naked before God, and then taking the truth we find there and inviting and nudging and pricking and confronting the world around us to undergo the same process. It's about understanding that we, the human species, are a body. When humans do something to each other, to the Earth, we are doing that. Us. It is our collective spiritual responsibility, and it is within our power to lift up an alternative, an alternative that is accessible right now, right here, to each and every one of us and to our global community as a whole. It's right here.

# Part 3: Dance party erupts in Quaker Meeting for Worship

When I left Guilford College, I left as a different Quaker than I was when I arrived. I was convinced of this path of visionary, confrontational love. Committing to that path had implications not just for my life but also for the lives of those around me and all of humanity, whose future I'm shaping with my actions every day. I realized that the word "Christ", the word "God", and the word "Spirit" have meaning to me, that they can help me navigate the world with this alternative understanding of power. Those concepts help me to steward the measure of light that is mine to carry. I still wrestle every day with the mainstream understanding of those words, and the way in which they have been usurped and distorted by some of the mainstream elements in my country. I don't want those manipulations to rob us of these essential spiritual tools.

I came back to my home communities after graduating from Guilford transformed, and I found myself alone. The Ashland Vineyard Community, Friends General Conference, and my friends from Baltimore Yearly Meeting had not undergone the same transformation that I had undergone. I found that some of the language I was using to describe my everyday life and my understanding of how I was making decisions and moving through the world felt off-putting to my home communities and, at times, downright alienating. I had a new challenge to wrestle with: maybe these were no longer my spiritual homes.

I felt frustrated by this new development. I had done all of this work to break out of my comfort zone, to stretch my understanding of Quakerism, and to realize the power and potential of this radical spiritual path. Yet, I was being told to bottle it up again because my language might make someone uncomfortable or because we "just don't talk about that".

I wrote the song "Friend Speaks My Mind" in an effort to talk about it—to reconcile the beauty of my upbringing (for which I am forever grateful) with this new understanding of the nature of Quakerism. The song was a love letter to my home communities at a time when I was feeling most alienated from them, and even (if I am being honest) a little judgmental about them.

The lyrics go something like this:

I found Quakers when I was just a kid. And now I'm studying them. I
hope you know how that is. I don't fully understand it. I don't know if
I can. But I understand enough to know that I am a fan. I mean, damn,
I didn't think that I would do this anymore. I didn't think that I would
do this anymore. I got bored. Listening to lectures felt like a chore but
now I'm begging Max Carter just to tell me some more. Oh, Lord.

And when I heard this Christian stuff, I'd get uncomfortable a lot.
I'm like, what does Jesus have to do with George Fox? And when I
heard the word Christ, it would make my jaw drop. But now I kind of
understand the man, I've got this soft spot.

I'm not a Christian, but I'm a Quaker. I've got Christ's inner light,
but he's not my savior. I'm on a date to meet my maker. I got down at
Young Friends with some funky behavior.
– "Friend Speaks My Mind", 2007

Of all the songs I have written, that's the one that goes viral? Oh, my
God.

We've made it back to 2009. I'm at the center of a lightning storm, and it's
not a lightning storm just about my song. It's a lightning storm that has been
brewing for over a century. It started in 1827 with the Hicksite–Orthodox
separation. It started with a letter from British Quaker Anna Braithwaite in
1824. It's a lightning storm that started when George Fox climbed Pendle
Hill and said there is a 'great people to be gathered'.

I want to take the question that my elder Scott Pierce-Coleman asked
me at Guilford College, and I want to ask it of all of you today, and I want to
ask it of every single person who commented on that video. You can say that
Quakerism is 'this' and Quakerism is 'that', but with whose authority do you
speak? What canst thou say?

# Part 4: Clothe Yourself in Righteousness

I want to tell you about the light-bulb moment, the moment that changed my understanding of Quakerism and the future, and how it led me to create a video series, which has attracted nearly five million views internationally, and now a brand-new 21$^{st}$-century Quaker media organization. But it would be remiss of me to skip over the project that occurred between these two programs, because it may offer the most meaning and insight into the future of the Religious Society of Friends as I imagine it.

That project is called "Clothe Yourself in Righteousness", and it's about one of my favorite early Quaker shenanigans, which they called 'going naked as a sign'. Those stories caught my attention when Max Carter told them, because as a college student, I knew a little bit about 'going naked as a sign'. Basically, we had a streaking club on Guilford campus. I don't know whether it's still a thing. Once a week, a big group of us would gather, take off our clothes and run a lap around the campus to blow off some steam.

For early Friends, going naked as a sign was something quite different. It was highly illegal to strip off one's clothes and run through the streets of London in 17th-century England. Anyone who did would be risking life and limb and family and property. Solomon Eccles, the Quaker I mentioned earlier, who burned his instruments—the same man who made shoes in the pulpit as a protest of the spiritual emptiness of the established church—went naked as a sign one morning in a busy market, called Smithfield Market, in central London. Solomon added a creative twist: a burning basket of brimstone on his head. That is usually the extent of the story, but in fact, Eccles had a heartbreaking reason, a devastating justification for doing this inexplicable thing, a justification I will share with you in just a moment.

In 2010, I received a call from my friend and fellow Guilfordian, Maggie Harrison. She was in seminary at the Earlham School of Religion, and she called me to say that she had a leading for me. If you know about leadings, you know that's not how it works, but if you knew Maggie, you would know why I went along with it. Maggie's leading was to explore the phenomenon of early Friends going naked: she would write a pamphlet, and I would record an album. I thought the idea was entertaining, so I started writing songs and Maggie began researching stories and theological writings.

I learned quickly that the project would be more than entertaining; it would be transformative. As it happened, the early Friends had some highly interesting reasons for feeling called to do this, and I would like to share three of those reasons with you.

# 1. Adam and Eve were ashamed

Quakers did not believe in the traditional interpretation of the story of Adam and Eve, who ate from the Tree of Knowledge and covered themselves upon realizing they were naked. Quakers told a different version: Adam and Eve were ashamed because they realized they had disobeyed God. They had been given a clear direction from their guide, who only wanted peace, truth and justice for them. And Adam and Eve had not honored that direction, which is why they put on clothing: to hide from God.

# 2. God is still speaking

In the Bible, there are several stories in which someone has a moment of divine inspiration, disrobes and walks naked through society. Early Quakers believed that if it happened in the Bible, it could happen during their time, too. The Bible was not a one and done thing. The story of the human species and our relationship with God is ongoing. It is an open book, much of which has yet to be written.

# 3. The Light is terrifying

The concept of the Light that I grew up with—the concept that we often refer to as Friends when we say we are 'holding someone in the Light' or when we refer to our own inner Light—feels like a warm glow of love, acceptance and affirmation. However, that is not how the early Quakers experienced it. For them, it was the 'refiner's fire', a burning spotlight of spiritual truth. When it shines on us, all of our discrepancies and inadequacies are revealed and burned away in a process that is as painful as it is revealing. We feel naked, stripped bare, exposed. But when we emerge from the experience, we are transformed: we are more pure, more full of love. We are reclothed, but not in worldly garments. Rather, we are clothed in righteousness.

This is the spiritual path that Friends believe in. It is not safe. It is not easy. It takes courage, and it cannot be done alone.

Back to Solomon Eccles and his naked march through Smithfield Market: it occurred during a period of great turmoil in England. On the heels of a civil war, the leadership of the country was unstable. A law had recently been passed making Quakerism illegal, revoking the freedom of religion. Citizens were forced to choose between attending the state-sanctioned Anglican Church on Sunday morning or risking arrest.

The Quakers, openly flouting the new law, were sitting in silent worship at the Bull and Mouth Meeting house on Aldersgate Street when constables burst in and broke up the Meeting. They swung batons as they worked their way through the worship space, injuring many Friends and killing at least one. The following day, Solomon Eccles made his way to Smithfield Market, stripped off his clothes, balanced a basket of brimstone on his head and walked the streets as a sign of the brokenness of the culture and the necessity to strip off these layers of violence, fear and worldly power.

> He says, 'I'm naked because we all are and God sees through this mess.
> Your identity's a farce—before birth and after death
> you're not a banker or a lawyer or a well-to-do man
> You're just another beggar with outstretched hands
> and you could fill them up with beauty
> you could fill them up with joy
> you could fill them up when times are rough with the glory of the Lord.
>
> But you wrap yourselves in linens
> and you wrap yourselves in silks
> and you wrap yourselves in blood and hell and guilt.'
> – "Smithfield Market pt 2", 2011

# Part 5: QuakerSpeak

Let's talk about this light bulb. We are living in a new era, in part shaped by a radical transformation in the way humans communicate with one another. I don't think anyone would debate that. An aspect of that new era means exposure to each other across geography and theology. It means a giant megaphone for those who know how to wield it. It means anyone with a combination of the right tools and lots of persistence, or who happens to be in the right place at the right time, can have an outsized influence. And the situation is constantly evolving. What is a precedent for that? I have one idea.

In the 17th century, when all those Quakers were running around engaging in their public shenanigans, the printing press was relatively new. The average person—the average community—had only recently gained access to it. Suddenly, anyone could print a tract, and the early Quakers were not shy about doing so. I recently interviewed Kate Peters, who wrote a book titled *Print Culture and the Early Quakers*, in which she writes that the early Quaker movement was 'a purposeful campaign which sought, and achieved, effective dialogue with both the body politic and society at large'.

Even more interestingly, the early Quakers were in their late teens and early twenties. They had grown up with this new publishing culture, and they understood it intuitively in ways their parents' generation could not. Here's what Kate had to say:

> Where the Quakers are interesting is that they're quite young. They're in their early twenties. It means that they've grown up in that—a bit like teenagers now with the internet. It's all they've known. So they turn quite naturally to it, and they're very savvy about how they're going to use print.
> – Kate Peters on *Thee Quaker Podcast*, Ep3: "Quakers and the Internet", 2023

When I look at the modern manifestation of the Religious Society of Friends, it's not surprising to me that we have not embraced social media and online video with the same gusto that the early Quakers embraced the printing press. Centuries of disagreement, quietism and complacency separate us from those bold, clear early Friends. But does that mean we have no voice? Has some spiritual DNA been passed down through those centuries that still

*27*

positions us as a spiritual people who can be bold? Do we still submit to being stripped of our worldly attachments and emerge speaking truth to power, even if our voice shakes?

We are missing a tremendous opportunity if we choose this moment to be unsure, half-hearted, or equivocal. This may be the greatest opportunity ever presented to Quakers and, more importantly, to the living truth that flows through us when we listen deeply. It's an opportunity to ignite that flame in each other. It is an opportunity to lift up our ministries, to deepen our practice and to confront those in the society around us, not as enemies but as brothers and sisters in God's love, each with the opportunity to get naked before God and be reclothed in righteousness.

Therefore, in 2013, I had an idea for a Quaker video project. It would be a YouTube channel with short, weekly interviews with Friends from all over the theological spectrum, answering not only the deepest, most fundamental questions about our faith but also the most superficial (Are we Amish? Do we all eat oats?) for an internet audience. For six years, I traveled, spoke with Friends from all over the world and published a weekly video.

The QuakerSpeak project was an experiment in exploring several questions: How can we use modern tools of communication to connect across national, cultural and theological divides? What is the legacy of short, intimate story-based communication for Friends and those interested in Friends? If Quakers publish messages on modern social-media platforms, messages that are crafted from the heart and from the Spirit but are not necessarily flashy, will anybody watch?

The answer to that last question unfolded over the course of six years, and it was a resounding 'yes'. My video project has now attracted nearly five million views. Wherever I travel, inevitably, someone approaches me and says, 'Hey, you're the guy from the end of the YouTube videos that helped me discover Quakerism.'

That is exciting to me. Someone who had been looking for something—even if they had not known what they were looking for—ended up finding it after I had a conversation with a Friend somewhere in the world and published it on YouTube.

And those six years of traveling and speaking with Friends did not just bring new eyes to the Religious Society of Friends—they changed my life. I heard stories that inspired me. I heard stories that challenged me and stories that expanded my idea of what it means to be a spiritual person and a Quaker in the 21st century.

Quakers believe that you can listen to someone in such a manner that their speaking changes. I have experienced this over and over again—even with cameras running and lights and microphones—when, as the interviewer, I have been in the zone. I cast my anxiety away and then make my whole body and Spirit a beacon, a channel for the love of God. Then, when I ask a question, I get a completely different answer than I would otherwise receive. It becomes a ministry.

I talked with one Quaker who participated in a sit-in during the Civil Rights Movement and who was threatened at knifepoint by a white supremacist. He looked the guy right in the eye and said, 'You do what you have to do, but I'm gonna try and love you while you do it.' I talked with a group of Quakers in Philadelphia who had sat silently in bank lobbies until PNC Bank reconsidered its investments in mountaintop coal mining. I interviewed a Friend who had staged a protest against the largest coal-burning power plant in New England by parking a tiny lobster boat in the way of a 40,000-ton coal shipment. He said he didn't know what was going to happen, but he knew this was his calling. True faithfulness is not about the outcome.

Whatever else we might think about the messages and theologies that someone shares, we can all feel it when they share from that place of deep listening and spiritual inspiration. I have learned that the world is hungry for this kind of listening and sharing, and it's something Quakers do well. That's why the project has five million views. Also—and not everybody knows this— Quakers are exciting. We might not move at the pace of society. But when we do something together, boldly and with clarity, we can move mountains. Or we can put them back.

# Part 6: Thee Quaker Project

Friends, the time has come for Quakers to step outside our comfort zone, to practice what we preach, and to preach what we practice. We are living through tremendously tumultuous times: our story is unfolding in the midst of political chaos and catastrophic climate change. This upheaval will continue to escalate throughout the 21$^{st}$ century. We remember that these problems have been created by humans, that Adam and Eve hid out of shame, not wisdom. We know who decides the future of the human race.

How can Friends rise to the occasion? Perhaps more importantly, what can we do to help support the next generation with the spiritual tools and the framework they will need in order to face the times ahead? We can look around us—as did the early Quakers—and say that this is an opportunity for the in-breaking of the kingdom of God. If the current world order is to be disrupted, then it is up to us, the living, to help shape the nature of that disruption. May we work together to create—with divine assistance—the beloved community here on earth.

I am not saying that all of us should feel called to internet ministries, or that these online forms should replace or supersede in-person ministries. As Friends, we know that we form a body. We have each been given a piece of the puzzle, and for each of us our job is to be as faithful to that piece as we can be. Each part of the body is different, so I am asking you to do the job that the Spirit has given you. Do it with courage. Do it with faithfulness. Do it once you are sure and after you have listened deeply with other Friends.

For my part, I know that the Spirit is not done with me. I know that five million views is not enough. It's barely scratching the surface. My experience of the early days of YouTube, my light-bulb moment, my experience at Guilford, my songwriting conviction, and my six years of interviewing Quakers have prepared me for something I never could have imagined when I first started on this path.

In the Spirit of Rufus Jones, of Clarence Pickett, of Jane Rushmore and of Henry Cadbury, I know that the Quakerism I have inherited is a gem, and it's up to my generation to carry it forward. It's up to us to treasure it, learn from it and update it.

After stepping back and evaluating the Quakerism I have inherited and what I now know about the 21$^{st}$ century, I am convinced that it is time for something bold and new and courageous—something updated for the times we are living through and responsive to the times we anticipate. Together with a group of Friends all across North America, I have been hard at work on this next leading: a brand new media organization whose goal is to explore the questions I have posed today, to tell stories of spiritual courage, and to give Quakers a platform on 21$^{st}$-century media. It's called "Thee Quaker Project".

Some would argue that the Religious Society of Friends is a relic without much to say in the 21$^{st}$ century. I would disagree with that, but, more importantly: it doesn't matter. Whether we as Quakers have something important to say has never mattered. What matters is that the Spirit has something to say. And, on our best days, with a lot of laborious love, we can give that Spirit a voice.

If we do still believe that we can channel the message of the Spirit to those willing to listen, and we believe the stakes are high (which they are), then let us not be afraid. The language may not always be the same, and the platform will be forever changing. But we know what we have been charged with: to lift up the Light given us, which is our portion, and carry it forward with courageous faithfulness.

---

Videos of some past lectures, including Jon Watts' presentation, can be accessed here: www.youtube.com/@quakersaustralia

# Notes

Manufactured by Amazon.com.au
Sydney, New South Wales, Australia